Hop-Frog

Courtly Cruelty & Fiery Revenge in a Macabre Tale of Triumph

A Modern Translation
Adapted for the Contemporary Reader

Edgar Allan Poe

Translated by Tim Zengerink

Table of Contents

Preface
Message to the Reader

Rebuilding the Greatest Library in Human History

Thousands of years ago, the Library of Alexandria was the heart of global knowledge — a sanctuary where the wisdom of every known civilization was gathered and shared freely.

And then, it was lost.

Now, we're rebuilding it — and you are invited to join us.

At the Library of Alexandria, we've set out to make every book available to every person on Earth — not just in print, but in every language, every format, and for every reader.

Here's how we do it:

- **Deluxe Print Editions at True Printing Cost** - Order any book as a high-quality paperback, elegant hardcover, or stunning boxset — and only pay what it costs to print. No markups. No middlemen.
- **Unlimited Access to the Greatest Works** - Enjoy thousands of timeless classics — from Plato to Shakespeare to Tolstoy — in beautiful, modern eBook and audiobook editions. Read and listen without limits — for every reader, everywhere.
- **Modern Translations for Every Language & Dialect** - We're reimagining the classics in clear, accessible language — and translating them into every dialect imaginable. Everyone deserves to understand humanity's greatest ideas.

When you visit **LibraryofAlexandria.com**, you're not just accessing books — you're joining a global movement to restore, preserve, and share the wisdom of civilization.

Join us today at LibraryofAlexandria.com

Together, we'll ensure the light of human wisdom never fades again.

With gratitude,

The Modern Library of Alexandria Team

Visit:
www.libraryofalexandria.com
Or scan the code below:

Introduction

Poe's Dark Allegory of Power, Cruelty, and Retribution

Among Edgar Allan Poe's many masterpieces of macabre storytelling, *Hop-Frog* (1849) occupies a unique and compelling place. Unlike some of Poe's more overtly psychological tales, *Hop-Frog* fuses a tightly constructed revenge narrative with elements of Gothic horror, grotesque humor, and sharp social critique. The story follows the plight of a court jester—nicknamed "*Hop-Frog*" due to his physical deformity—who is subjected to the relentless cruelty of a tyrannical king and his seven ministers. Through a cunning and horrifying act of revenge, the jester transforms from a victim of ridicule and abuse into a terrifying figure of justice, reclaiming his dignity in a single, fiery moment of triumph.

First published in *The Flag of Our Union* in March 1849, *Hop-Frog* was one of the last stories Poe wrote before his death later that year. It stands as a distillation of his lifelong fascination with themes of oppression, humiliation, and the dark potential of human ingenuity when pushed to its limits. Like many of Poe's works, the story operates on multiple levels. It can be read as a simple tale of revenge—a servant who outwits and destroys his cruel masters—or as a deeper allegory about the abuse of power, the dehumanization of those deemed "lesser," and the explosive consequences of unchecked tyranny.

The titular character, *Hop-Frog*, is a dwarf and a cripple, physically disadvantaged but endowed with a sharp mind, creative intelligence, and a capacity for calculated vengeance. His role as a jester places him in a paradoxical position: he is both central to the court's entertainment and entirely excluded from its power structures. His only friend and ally is Trippetta, a fellow dwarf, whose grace and beauty contrast with his own physical hardships. Together, they navigate a world of ridicule and casual cruelty, their humanity constantly overshadowed by the whims of the king and his sycophantic courtiers. When Trippetta is publicly humiliated—struck and degraded by the king—*Hop-Frog*'s slow-burning resentment ignites into a carefully orchestrated plan for revenge.

Poe's narrative unfolds with his characteristic precision, building tension through subtle details and psychological insights. The court, with its obsession with spectacle and masquerade, becomes the perfect stage for *Hop-Frog*'s final act. The king and his ministers, eager to indulge in elaborate entertainments, fall prey to *Hop-Frog*'s suggestion of appearing as chained orangutans during a grand masquerade. Their decision, meant to inspire laughter and shock among the courtiers, instead seals their fate. In a scene of unforgettable horror, *Hop-Frog* traps them, douses them with tar and flax, and sets them ablaze before the assembled court, delivering poetic justice in a fiery and unforgettable finale.

Themes of Humiliation, Revenge, and Justice

At the heart of *Hop-Frog* lies a profound meditation on the dynamics of power and cruelty. The king and his ministers treat *Hop-Frog* and Trippetta not as individuals with feelings and intelligence but as objects of amusement, mocking their appearances and exploiting their talents for courtly entertainment. This dehumanization is emblematic of a broader social commentary: Poe critiques the tendency of those in power to regard others—particularly those who are physically different or socially disadvantaged—as mere instruments for their own gratification.

Hop-Frog's revenge, though brutal, is framed as an act of justice. It is not random or mindless violence but a meticulously planned response to years of humiliation, culminating in the ultimate punishment of those who mocked and abused him. Through this lens, Poe invites readers to question the fine line between justice and vengeance. Is *Hop-Frog*'s act of setting the king and his ministers ablaze an overreach, or is it the only means by which he can reclaim his humanity and agency? The story's chilling conclusion suggests that in a world where cruelty is unchecked, vengeance becomes a natural, if horrifying, form of redress.

The figure of Trippetta adds another layer of complexity to the story. Though she plays a less active role than *Hop-Frog*, her presence underscores the themes of loyalty, compassion, and solidarity among the oppressed. It is her public humiliation that triggers *Hop-Frog*'s final act, making the story not just one of personal revenge but also of defending the dignity of those who cannot defend themselves. The bond between *Hop-Frog* and Trippetta serves as a counterpoint to the cruelty of the court, highlighting the human capacity for empathy even in the face of relentless ridicule.

Another significant theme in *Hop-Frog* is the role of performance and disguise. The masquerade ball, a recurring motif in Poe's work (seen also in *The Masque of the Red Death*), becomes a space where identities are fluid and appearances can deceive. The king and his ministers, dressed as orangutans, intend to provoke fear and amusement, but they themselves become the victims of a far deadlier performance. *Hop-Frog*, who has spent his life forced to entertain others, seizes control of the stage, turning the tools of performance into instruments of retribution. In this sense, the story can be seen as a narrative about the power of art and creativity—not as mere amusement, but as a force capable of profound transformation and justice.

Poe's Style and the Reader's Experience

Poe's prose in *Hop-Frog* is sharp, vivid, and deliberate, blending moments of grotesque humor with a steadily mounting sense of dread. His descriptions of the court's excesses—the king's gluttony, the courtiers' sycophancy, the obsession with elaborate costumes—are tinged with both satire and horror. Through carefully crafted language, Poe paints a picture of a world that is at once decadent and cruel, where the powerful indulge their whims at the expense of the vulnerable. The story's climactic scene, in which the king and his ministers are set on fire, is described with a stark, almost clinical intensity that heightens its impact.

One of Poe's most striking narrative techniques in *Hop-Frog* is his use of contrasts: between the physical weakness of the jester and the strength of his intellect; between the gaiety of the masquerade and the horror of its conclusion; between the cruelty of the king and the righteousness of *Hop-Frog*'s vengeance. These contrasts create a dynamic tension that keeps readers engaged while also underscoring the story's moral and thematic weight.

Hop-Frog also reflects Poe's interest in the psychology of oppression and revenge. The titular character is not portrayed simply as a victim or a hero but as a complex figure whose intelligence and creativity have been sharpened by suffering. His transformation from jester to avenger is both shocking and satisfying, as it fulfills the narrative arc of a character who has long been denied respect and agency. Yet there is also an undercurrent of unease: the violence of *Hop-Frog*'s revenge forces readers to confront their own feelings about justice, cruelty, and the desire for retribution.

For contemporary readers, *Hop-Frog* remains as relevant and thought-provoking as it was in Poe's time. The story's exploration of power dynamics, the abuse of authority, and the resilience of the oppressed resonates across cultures and eras. It serves as both a cautionary tale about the dangers of dehumanization and a dark celebration of the human spirit's capacity to overcome adversity through intelligence and willpower.

As you read *Hop-Frog*, consider the multiple layers of meaning that Poe weaves into this brief but powerful tale. It is a story about more than revenge; it is about the reclaiming of voice and agency in a world that seeks to silence and mock those who are different. Through its blend of horror, satire, and moral complexity, *Hop-Frog* invites readers to reflect on the nature of justice, the consequences of cruelty, and the transformative power of wit and courage.

Hop-Frog

I had never encountered anyone who appreciated humor as intensely as the king did. He appeared to exist solely for the purpose of making jokes. Sharing an excellent humorous tale, and delivering it skillfully, was the most reliable path to earning his approval. Consequently, all seven of his ministers were renowned for their talents as comedians. They also resembled the king in being tall, heavy-set, well-fed men, in addition to being exceptional jokesters. Whether individuals become overweight from constant joking, or whether there exists something inherent in being overweight that naturally inclines one toward humor, I have never been able to fully determine; however, it is certainly true that a thin comedian is an extremely rare phenomenon.

About the refinements, or what he called the "ghost" of wit, the king cared very little. He particularly admired boldness in a joke and would often tolerate lengthy ones for that quality alone. Excessive subtleties tired him. He would have chosen Rabelais' "Gargantua" over Voltaire's "Zadig," and overall, physical pranks appealed to his taste much more than clever wordplay.

At the time of my story, professional jesters hadn't completely disappeared from royal courts. Many of the major European "powers" still kept their "fools," who dressed in colorful patchwork clothing with caps and bells, and who were supposed to always have clever jokes ready at a moment's notice, in exchange for the scraps that dropped from the king's table.

Our king naturally kept his "fool." The truth is, he needed some form of foolishness—if only to balance out the weighty wisdom of the seven wise men who served as his ministers—not to mention his own wisdom.

His fool, or professional jester, was more than just a fool, though. The king valued him three times as much because he was also a dwarf and disabled. In those days, dwarfs were just as common at court as fools were, and many rulers would have struggled to get through their days (court days tend to be much longer than anywhere else) without both a jester to laugh with and a dwarf to laugh at. But as I've already mentioned, jesters are fat, round, and clumsy ninety-nine times out of a hundred—so our king took great pride in the fact that with Hop-Frog (that was the fool's name), he had a triple treasure all in one person.

I believe the name "Hop-Frog" wasn't the name given to the dwarf by his godparents at his baptism, but rather it was bestowed upon him through the unanimous agreement of the seven ministers because of his inability to walk like other people. In reality, Hop-Frog could only move around using a kind of jerky gait—something that fell between a jump and a squirm—a way of moving that provided endless entertainment, and naturally great satisfaction, to the king, because (despite his protruding belly and his naturally swollen head) the king was considered by his entire court to be an excellent specimen.

While Hop-Frog could only move with tremendous pain and difficulty across roads or floors due to his deformed legs, nature appeared to have given him extraordinary muscular strength in his arms to make up for what his lower limbs lacked, allowing him to accomplish remarkable feats of agility when it came to trees, ropes, or anything else that required climbing. During such activities, he definitely looked much more like a squirrel or a small monkey than a frog.

I cannot say exactly which country Hop-Frog originally came from. It was from some uncivilized region, however, that no one had ever heard of—a great distance from our king's court. Hop-Frog, and a young girl who was almost as small as he was (though she had perfect proportions and was an amazing dancer), had been forcibly taken from their homes in neighboring provinces and given as gifts to the king by one of his always-victorious generals.

Given these circumstances, it's not surprising that the two little prisoners developed a close bond. They quickly became devoted friends. Hop-Frog, who provided plenty of entertainment but wasn't well-liked, couldn't offer Trippetta much help; however, she was universally loved and spoiled because of her elegance and stunning beauty (despite being a dwarf), which gave her considerable influence; and she always used that power, whenever possible, to help Hop-Frog.

On some grand state occasion—I can't remember what—the king decided to hold a masquerade, and whenever a masquerade or anything of that sort took place at our court, the talents of both Hop-Frog and Trippetta were certain to be put to use. Hop-Frog, in particular, was so creative when it came to organizing pageants, proposing new characters, and designing costumes for masked balls, that it seemed nothing could be accomplished without his help.

The night chosen for the celebration had come. Under Trippetta's supervision, a magnificent hall had been decorated with every possible ornament that could bring splendor to a masquerade. The entire court buzzed with anticipation. When it came to costumes and characters, one would naturally assume that everyone had made their decisions on these matters. Many people had decided what roles they would play a week, or even a month, beforehand; and indeed, there wasn't a trace of uncertainty anywhere—except when it came to the king and his seven ministers. I could never understand why they wavered, unless they were doing it as some kind of joke. More likely, they found it challenging to make up their minds because of how overweight they were. In any case, time passed quickly; and as a final option, they called for Trippetta and Hop-Frog.

When the two little friends responded to the king's call, they discovered him drinking wine with the seven members of his cabinet council; however, the monarch seemed to be in a terrible mood. He was well aware that Hop-Frog disliked wine, since it drove the poor cripple nearly to madness; and madness brings no comfort. Yet the king enjoyed his practical jokes and delighted in forcing Hop-Frog to drink and (as the king put it) "to be merry."

"Come here, Hop-Frog," he said as the jester and his friend entered the room. "Drink this full glass to the health of your absent friends," he continued, and here Hop-Frog sighed. "Then give us the benefit of your creativity. We need characters—characters, man—something new and different. We're tired of this constant repetition. Come on, drink! The wine will sharpen your mind."

Hop-Frog tried, as he always did, to come up with a joke in response to the king's remarks, but the attempt was too difficult for him. It was the unfortunate dwarf's birthday, and being ordered to drink to his "absent friends" brought tears to his eyes. Several large, bitter tears dropped into the cup as he accepted it meekly from the tyrant's hand.

"Ah! ha! ha! ha!" the man burst out laughing as the dwarf reluctantly emptied the cup. "Look what a glass of good wine can accomplish! Your eyes are already sparkling!"

Poor fellow! His large eyes gleamed rather than shone, because the wine's effect on his excitable mind was both powerful and immediate. He nervously set the goblet down on the table and looked around at the group with a half-crazed stare. Everyone appeared highly entertained by the success of the king's 'joke.'

"And now let's get down to business," said the prime minister, a very heavy-set man.

"Yes," said the King. "Come, Hop-Frog, give us your help. Characters, my good fellow; we need characters—all of us—ha! ha! ha!" Since this was seriously intended as a joke, his laughter was echoed by the seven.

Hop-Frog laughed as well, though his laughter was weak and somewhat empty.

"Come on, come on," said the king impatiently, "don't you have anything to suggest?"

"I'm trying to think of something new," the dwarf replied, distracted, since he was completely confused by the wine.

"Trying!" the tyrant shouted angrily. "What do you mean by that? Ah, I see. You're being moody and want more wine. Here, drink this!" He poured another full cup and held it out to the disabled man, who simply stared at it while struggling to breathe.

"Drink, I say!" shouted the monster, "or by the fiends"

The dwarf paused uncertainly. The king's face turned deep purple with fury. The courtiers sneered with amusement. Trippetta, white as death, moved toward the monarch's throne, and dropping to her knees in front of him, begged him to show mercy to her friend.

The tyrant stared at her for several moments, clearly amazed by her boldness. He appeared completely uncertain about what to do or say—how to properly express his anger.

Finally, without speaking a word, he shoved her roughly away from him and threw the contents of the full cup in her face.

The poor girl got up as best she could, and without daring even to sigh, returned to her position at the foot of the table.

There was complete silence for about thirty seconds, during which you could have heard a leaf or feather drop. The quiet was broken by a low, harsh, grinding sound that dragged on and seemed to come from every corner of the room at the same time.

"What—what—what are you making that noise for?" the king demanded, turning furiously toward the dwarf.

The man appeared to have largely sobered up from his drunken state, and staring steadily but calmly into the dictator's face, simply said:

"I—I? How could it have been me?"

"The sound seemed to come from outside," one of the courtiers remarked. "I believe it was the parrot at the window, sharpening his beak on the bars of his cage."

"That's right," the king responded, seeming greatly relieved by the explanation; "but I swear on my honor as a knight, I could have sworn it was the grinding of this scoundrel's teeth."

At this, the dwarf burst into laughter (the king was such a dedicated jester that he didn't mind anyone laughing), and revealed a set of large, strong, and quite disgusting teeth. Furthermore, he declared his complete readiness to drink as much wine as anyone wanted. The king was satisfied; and after downing another full glass without any noticeable bad effects, Hop-Frog immediately and enthusiastically joined in the planning for the masquerade.

"I can't explain what triggered the thought," he remarked, speaking very calmly as if he had never touched alcohol in his entire life, "but right after your majesty struck the girl and threw the wine in her face—right after your majesty did this, and while the parrot was making that strange sound outside the window, an excellent entertainment came to mind—one of my own country's amusements—frequently performed among us at our costume parties: but here it would be completely new. Unfortunately, though, it needs a group of eight people and—"

"Here we are!" exclaimed the king, laughing at his sharp realization of the coincidence; "eight exactly—myself and my seven ministers. Come! What entertainment do you have for us?"

"We call it," the disabled man replied, "the Eight Chained Orangutans, and it's truly excellent entertainment when performed well."

"We will make it happen," the king declared, straightening his posture and narrowing his eyes.

"The beauty of the game," continued Hop-Frog, "lies in the terror it creates among the women."

"Excellent!" shouted the monarch and his ministry together.

"I'll dress you up as orangutans," the dwarf continued; "just leave everything to me. The resemblance will be so convincing that the masquerade party guests will think you're actual animals—and naturally, they'll be just as frightened as they are amazed."

"Oh, this is perfect!" the king exclaimed. "Hop-Frog! I will make a man of you."

"The chains are meant to create more chaos with their clanking sound. You're supposed to have broken free as a

13

group from your captors. Your majesty can't imagine the impact created at a masquerade ball by eight chained orangutans that most of the guests believe are real, bursting in with wild screams among the crowd of elegantly and magnificently dressed men and women. The contrast is beyond comparison."

"It has to be," the king declared, and the council quickly stood up (since it was getting late) to carry out Hop-Frog's plan.

His method of dressing up the group as orangutans was quite simple, yet it worked perfectly for what he had in mind. At the time this story takes place, these animals were almost never seen anywhere in the civilized world; and since the dwarf's costumes looked convincingly animal-like and were more than frightening enough, people would naturally assume they were authentic representations of the real creatures.

The king and his ministers were first dressed in tight-fitting undershirts and underwear made of stretchy fabric. They were then completely soaked with tar. At this point in the process, someone in the group suggested using feathers, but the dwarf immediately rejected this idea, quickly convincing all eight men through visual proof that the fur of a creature like an orangutan would be much better represented by flax fibers. A thick layer of flax was then spread over the tar coating. A long chain was brought over. First, it was wrapped around the king's waist and secured; then around another member of the group, and also secured; then around each person in turn, using the same method. When this chaining system was finished, and the group stood as far away from each other as the chain allowed, they formed a circle; and to make everything look realistic, Hop-Frog ran the remaining length of chain across the circle in two straight lines at right angles to each other, following the same technique used today by people who capture chimpanzees or other large apes in Borneo.

The grand ballroom where the masquerade was to be held was a circular room with very high ceilings that received sunlight only through a single window at the top. During the evening hours (the time for which the room was specifically designed) it was lit mainly by a large chandelier that hung from a chain attached to the center of the skylight, and could be raised or lowered using a counterweight system as was typical; however (to avoid an unattractive appearance) this counterweight mechanism ran outside the dome and across the roof.

Trippetta had been put in charge of arranging the room, but it appeared that in certain details, she had followed the more level-headed advice of her dwarf friend. It was at his suggestion that the chandelier had been taken down for this event. The wax that would inevitably drip from it in such warm weather would have seriously damaged the expensive clothing of the guests, who couldn't all be expected to stay away from the center of the crowded ballroom—that is, from directly beneath where the chandelier would hang. Instead, extra wall sconces had been installed in different areas of the hall, positioned safely out of the way, and a sweet-smelling torch had been placed in the right hand of each of the Caryatides that lined the walls—about fifty or sixty of them in total.

The eight orangutans, following Hop-Frog's advice, waited patiently until midnight when the room was completely packed with costumed party-goers before making their entrance. As soon as the clock finished striking twelve, they rushed in—or more accurately, tumbled in all at once—since their chains were so cumbersome that most of the group fell down, and everyone stumbled as they came through the door.

The excitement among the party guests was enormous, and it filled the king's heart with delight. As expected, quite a few of the guests believed the fierce-looking creatures were actually real animals of some sort, if not exactly orangutans. Many of the women fainted from terror; and if the king hadn't taken the precaution of banning all weapons from the ballroom, his party might have quickly paid for their prank with their lives. As things stood, everyone made a frantic rush toward the doors; but the king had ordered them to be locked immediately after his entrance; and, following the dwarf's suggestion, the keys had been left in his possession.

While the chaos reached its peak, and each costumed party-goer focused only on their own safety (since there was genuine danger from the pressure of the agitated crowd), the chain that normally held the chandelier, which had been pulled up when the fixture was removed, could be seen slowly lowering until its hooked end came within three feet of the floor.

Soon after this happened, the king and his seven friends had stumbled around the hall in every direction and eventually found themselves in the center, which naturally brought them into direct contact with the chain. While they stood in this position, the dwarf had silently followed behind them, encouraging them to continue their wild behavior, and grabbed their chain where the two sections crossed the circle at opposite ends and formed right angles. At this spot, moving as quick as lightning, he attached the hook that had previously held the chandelier; instantly, through some hidden mechanism, the chandelier chain was pulled so high that the hook became unreachable, and as an unavoidable result, this forced the orangutans to be dragged together into tight contact, standing face to face.

By this time, the costumed party guests had somewhat recovered from their shock and were starting to see the whole situation as an elaborate joke, so they burst into loud laughter at the predicament of the apes.

"Leave them to me!" Hop-Frog shouted, his piercing voice cutting through all the noise. "Leave them to me. I think I recognize them. If I can just get a clear view of them, I'll be able to tell you who they are right away."

Here, climbing over the heads of the crowd, he managed to reach the wall; then, grabbing a torch from one of the Caryatides, he made his way back, as he had come, to the center of the room—jumped, with the nimbleness of a monkey, onto the king's head, and from there climbed a few feet up the chain; holding the torch down to examine the group of orangutans, and still shouting: "I shall soon find out who they are!"

And now, while the entire gathering (including the apes) was doubled over with laughter, the jester suddenly let out a piercing whistle; at that moment the chain shot violently upward about thirty feet—pulling along the terrified and thrashing orangutans, leaving them hanging in the air between the skylight and the floor. Hop-Frog, gripping the chain as it ascended, kept his position relative to the eight masked figures, and continued (as if nothing had happened) to push his torch down toward them, as though trying to figure out who they were.

The entire group was so completely amazed by this sudden rise that they fell into complete silence for about a minute. The quiet was interrupted by the same low, rough, scraping noise that had earlier caught the attention of the king and his advisors when the king had thrown wine in

17

Trippetta's face. But this time, there was no doubt about where the sound was coming from. It emerged from the sharp, pointed teeth of the dwarf, who was grinding and gnashing them together while foam gathered at his mouth, and he stared with a look of wild fury at the upturned faces of the king and his seven companions.

"Ah, ha!" the furious jester finally exclaimed. "Ah, ha! Now I'm starting to understand who these people really are!" At this point, pretending to examine the king more carefully, he brought the torch close to the flax-covered costume that wrapped around him, which immediately erupted into a brilliant sheet of flame. In under thirty seconds, all eight of the orangutans were burning intensely, while the crowd below watched in terror, screaming and completely unable to offer any help whatsoever.

At last the flames, suddenly growing more intense, forced the jester to climb higher up the chain to escape their reach; and as he made this movement, the crowd fell silent again for a brief moment. The dwarf seized his opportunity and spoke once more:

"I can now see clearly," he said, "what kind of people these masked figures really are. They are a powerful king and his seven closest advisors—a king who doesn't hesitate to hit a defenseless girl and his seven counselors who help him commit this terrible act. As for me, I am simply Hop-Frog, the jester—and this is my final joke."

Because both the flax and the tar it stuck to were highly flammable, the dwarf had barely finished his short speech when his revenge was complete. The eight bodies hung in their chains, now a foul-smelling, charred, grotesque, and unrecognizable mass. The cripple threw his torch at them, climbed slowly to the ceiling, and vanished through the skylight.

It's believed that Trippetta, positioned on the roof of the ballroom, had been her friend's partner in his fiery revenge, and that together they managed to escape to their homeland, since neither was ever seen again.

THE MAN OF THE CROWD.

"This great misfortune, of not being able to be alone."—La Bruyère.

Someone once made an astute observation about a particular German book that "er lasst sich nicht lesen"—it refuses to allow itself to be read. There are certain secrets that simply will not allow themselves to be spoken. Men pass away in the darkness of night in their beds, clutching the hands of spiritual confessors and gazing at them with pleading eyes—dying with hearts full of despair and throats seized by convulsions, all because of the terrible nature of mysteries that refuse to let themselves be exposed. Occasionally, unfortunately, a person's conscience becomes burdened with something so overwhelmingly horrific that it can only be cast off by taking it to the grave. And so the true nature of all wrongdoing remains forever hidden.

Not long ago, on an autumn evening as darkness was falling, I sat by the large curved window of the D—— Coffee-House in London. For several months I had been suffering from poor health, but I was now recovering, and with my returning strength, I found myself in one of those delightful states of mind that are the complete opposite of boredom—moods of the sharpest eagerness, when the fog lifts from one's mental vision—the αχλυξ η πριν επῆευ—and the mind, energized, exceeds its ordinary condition as greatly as Leibnitz's brilliant yet honest reasoning surpasses the wild and shallow rhetoric of Gorgias. Simply breathing was a pleasure; and I found genuine enjoyment even in many things that would normally cause distress. I felt a peaceful but curious interest in everything around me. With a cigar between my lips and a newspaper resting on my lap, I had been entertaining myself for most of the afternoon, sometimes studying the advertisements closely, sometimes watching the diverse crowd in the room, and sometimes gazing through the smoky glass panes out into the street.

This street is one of the main roads through the city, and it had been extremely busy all day long. However, as night began to fall, the crowds grew even larger; and by the time the streetlights were fully lit, two thick and steady streams of people were flowing past the entrance. I had never found myself in such a situation at this particular time of evening before, and the chaotic ocean of human heads filled me with a wonderful sense of new excitement. Eventually, I stopped paying attention to everything happening inside the hotel and became completely absorbed in watching the scene outside.

Initially, my observations were abstract and broad in scope. I viewed the passengers as groups and considered them in terms of their collective characteristics. Before long, though, I shifted my focus to specifics, examining with careful attention the countless variations in body shape, clothing, demeanor, walking style, facial features, and expressions.

Most of the people passing by had a confident, business-focused appearance and seemed concerned only with making their way through the crowd. Their foreheads were furrowed, and their eyes moved rapidly; when bumped into by other pedestrians, they showed no signs of irritation but simply straightened their clothing and continued hurrying along. Another group, still quite large in number, moved restlessly with reddened faces, talking and gesturing to themselves as if they felt isolated despite being surrounded by so many people. When their progress was blocked, these individuals would suddenly stop their mumbling but increase their hand movements, waiting with a distracted and exaggerated smile on their faces for whoever was blocking them to move on. If someone bumped into them, they would bow repeatedly to those who had jostled them and seemed completely flustered. There wasn't anything particularly remarkable about these two major groups beyond what I've described. Their clothing belonged to the category that is specifically called respectable. They were certainly aristocrats, businessmen, lawyers, shopkeepers, stockbrokers—the elite and the ordinary members of society—people with free time and those actively involved in their own business matters—handling affairs under their own authority. They didn't particularly capture my interest.

The group of office workers was an easy one to spot, and within it I noticed two distinct categories. There were the junior clerks from fashionable establishments—young men wearing fitted jackets, polished boots, slicked-back hair, and wearing expressions of superiority. Apart from a certain stylish way of carrying themselves, which could be called desk-worker swagger for lack of a better term, these people's behavior struck me as an exact copy of what had been considered the height of fashion about twelve to eighteen months earlier. They displayed the discarded elegance of the upper class—and this, I believe, captures the best description of this group.

The senior clerks from established firms, or the "reliable old-timers," were impossible to miss. You could recognize them by their black or brown coats and trousers, tailored for comfort, paired with white neckties and vests, sturdy-looking shoes, and thick stockings or leg coverings.

They all had somewhat balding heads, and their right ears, accustomed to years of holding pens, had developed the peculiar tendency to stick out. I noticed they always adjusted or removed their hats using both hands, and they carried pocket watches attached to short gold chains of solid, old-fashioned design. They embodied an air of respectability—if such a display can truly be called pretentious when it carries such dignity.

There were many people with flashy appearances, and I could easily tell they belonged to the group of well-dressed pickpockets that plague all major cities. I observed these individuals with great curiosity, and found it hard to understand how they could ever be mistaken for gentlemen by actual gentlemen. Their oversized shirt cuffs, combined with an overly bold manner, should give them away immediately.

The gamblers, of whom I spotted quite a few, were even easier to identify. They wore all kinds of clothing, from the desperate con artist's outfit with velvet vest, decorative scarf, gold chains, and ornate buttons, to the carefully plain clergyman's attire, which couldn't look less suspicious. Yet all were marked by a certain bloated darkness of skin, a cloudy dullness in their eyes, and pale, tight-pressed lips. There were two other characteristics, furthermore, by which I could always spot them: a carefully quiet way of speaking, and an unusually wide spread of the thumb extending at right angles to the fingers. Very often, alongside these swindlers, I noticed a group of men somewhat different in their ways, but still cut from the same cloth. They can be described as gentlemen who make their living through cunning. They seem to exploit the public in two divisions— the fashionable dandies and the military types. The first group's main features are flowing hair and constant smiles;

the second group's are decorated military coats and perpetual scowls.

Moving down through the levels of what people call respectability, I discovered darker and more profound subjects to contemplate. I observed Jewish peddlers, their sharp eyes gleaming from faces where every other feature showed nothing but complete submissiveness; tough professional street beggars glaring at higher-class panhandlers who had been forced out into the night by desperation alone to seek charity; weak and pale invalids who were clearly marked for death, shuffling and stumbling through the crowd while looking pleadingly at everyone's face, as though searching for some random comfort or lost hope; humble young women walking home from long hours of late work to cold, unwelcoming houses, shrinking more in fear than anger from the stares of criminals whose physical presence they couldn't even escape; prostitutes of every type and age—the unmistakable beauty in her prime, reminding me of the statue described by Lucian, with a surface like pristine marble but an interior full of corruption—the disgusting and completely ruined diseased woman in tatters—the wrinkled, jewelry-covered, makeup-smeared old woman making one final attempt at appearing young—the mere child with an undeveloped body who had already become skilled in the terrible seductive arts of her profession through long exposure, burning with fierce desire to be considered equal to her older colleagues in corruption; countless and indescribable drunkards—some in torn rags, staggering and unable to speak clearly, with battered faces and dull eyes—some wearing complete but dirty clothes, walking with a slightly unsteady swagger, thick sensual lips, and healthy-looking red faces—others dressed in materials that had once been fine and were still carefully brushed—men who walked with an unnaturally firm and energetic step, but whose faces were terrifyingly pale, whose eyes were horribly wild and bloodshot, and who grabbed with trembling fingers at every object within reach as they pushed through the crowd; alongside these, pie sellers, porters, coal carriers, chimney sweeps; organ grinders, monkey trainers, and ballad sellers, those who sold mingling with those who performed; ragged craftsmen and worn-out workers of every kind, all filled with a loud and excessive energy that clashed harshly on the ears and created a painful sensation for the eyes.

As the night grew deeper, my fascination with the scene intensified as well. The crowd's overall character changed dramatically—its more refined qualities disappeared as the respectable people gradually left, while its rougher elements became more prominent as the late hour drew out every kind of criminal from their hiding places. Meanwhile, the gas lamps, which had initially struggled weakly against the fading daylight, finally took control and cast everything in an unsteady, harsh glow. Everything appeared dark yet magnificent—like the ebony that writers have compared to Tertullian's literary style.

The dramatic effects of the light captivated me, drawing my attention to examine individual faces; and even though the speed at which this world of light flickered past the window prevented me from doing more than glancing at each face, it still seemed that, in my particular state of mind at that moment, I could often read, even in that brief moment of a glance, the story of many years.

With my forehead pressed against the glass, I was busy studying the crowd when suddenly a face came into view— that of a worn-out old man, around sixty-five or seventy years old. This face immediately caught and completely captured my attention because of the utterly unique quality of its expression. I had never seen anything even remotely similar to that expression before. I clearly recall that my first thought upon seeing it was that Retzch, if he had witnessed it, would have much preferred it to his own artistic representations of the devil. As I tried, during the short moment of my initial observation, to understand the meaning behind what I saw, there arose chaotically and contradictorily in my mind the concepts of enormous mental strength, of wariness, of stinginess, of greed, of coldness, of hatred, of bloodlust, of victory, of joy, of extreme terror, of intense—of absolute despair. I felt strangely excited, shocked, captivated. "What a wild story," I told myself, "is written within that chest!" Then came an urgent desire to keep the man in sight—to learn more about him. Quickly putting on an overcoat and grabbing my hat and walking stick, I made my way onto the street and pushed through the crowd in the direction I had seen him go, since he had already vanished. With some difficulty I finally spotted him again, got closer, and followed him closely but carefully, so as not to draw his attention.

I now had a perfect chance to study his appearance. He was short, extremely thin, and seemed very weak. His clothing was generally dirty and torn; but whenever he passed under the bright light of a street lamp, I noticed that his shirt, though soiled, was made of fine fabric. Unless my eyes were playing tricks on me, through a tear in the tightly buttoned and obviously secondhand cloak that wrapped around him, I caught sight of both a diamond and a dagger. These details sparked my curiosity even more, and I decided to follow this stranger wherever he might lead.

Night had completely fallen, and a thick, humid fog settled over the city, which soon turned into steady, heavy rain. This weather change had a strange effect on the crowd, causing everyone to suddenly stir into new activity as they were covered by a sea of umbrellas. The swaying, pushing, and buzzing sounds increased ten times over. As for me, I didn't pay much attention to the rain—an old fever lingering in my body made the moisture feel somewhat dangerously pleasant. I tied a handkerchief around my mouth and continued on. For half an hour, the old man struggled to make his way along the main street, and I walked close beside him, afraid I might lose sight of him. He never turned his head to look back, so he didn't notice me. Eventually, he turned into a side street that, while still packed with people, wasn't quite as crowded as the main street he had left. Here, a change in his behavior became obvious. He walked more slowly and with less purpose than before—more hesitantly. He crossed back and forth across the street repeatedly with no clear goal, and the crowd was still so thick that with every movement he made, I had to follow him closely. The street was narrow and long, and he spent nearly an hour walking through it, during which time the number of people gradually decreased to about what you'd normally see at noon on Broadway near the park—showing the vast difference between a London crowd and that of the busiest American city. A second turn brought us into a square that was brightly lit and bursting with activity. The stranger's old behavior returned. His chin dropped to his chest while his eyes darted wildly from beneath his furrowed brows in every direction, looking at those who surrounded him. He pushed his way forward steadily and persistently. I was surprised, however, to discover that after he had walked around the entire square, he turned around and retraced his steps. I was even more amazed to see him repeat the same walk several times—once nearly catching me when he came around with a sudden movement.

In this exercise he spent another hour, and by the end we encountered much less interference from pedestrians than we had initially. The rain was coming down hard, the air had turned cool, and people were heading back to their homes. With an impatient gesture, the wanderer turned into a side street that was relatively empty. Down this street, which stretched about a quarter of a mile, he hurried with an energy I never could have imagined seeing in someone so old, and which caused me considerable difficulty in keeping up. Within a few minutes we arrived at a large and bustling marketplace, with which the stranger seemed thoroughly familiar, and where his original behavior became evident once again, as he pushed his way back and forth, without purpose, among the crowd of buyers and sellers.

During the hour and a half or so that we spent in this area, I had to be extremely careful to stay close enough to observe him without drawing his attention. Fortunately, I was wearing rubber overshoes and could move around completely silently. At no point did he notice that I was watching him. He went into store after store, didn't ask about prices for anything, said nothing, and stared at everything with a wild and empty expression. I was now completely baffled by his behavior and determined that we wouldn't separate until I had learned something meaningful about him.

A clock with a booming voice struck eleven, and people were quickly leaving the bazaar. As a shopkeeper put up his shutter, he bumped into the old man, and at that moment I witnessed a violent tremor pass through his body. He rushed into the street, glanced around nervously for a moment, and then ran with amazing speed through numerous winding and empty lanes, until we came out again onto the main road where we had begun—the street of the D—— Hotel. However, it no longer had the same appearance. It was still brightly lit with gas lamps; but the rain poured down heavily, and few people could be seen. The stranger turned pale. He walked gloomily for several steps up the once crowded avenue, then, with a deep sigh, turned toward the river, and, pushing through many different winding paths, eventually came within sight of one of the major theaters. It was about to close, and the audience was pouring out through the doors. I saw the old man gasp as though struggling for air while he threw himself into the crowd; but I believed that the terrible anguish on his face had somewhat lessened. His head dropped to his chest again; he looked as I had first seen him. I noticed that he now followed the path taken by most of the audience—but overall, I couldn't understand the unpredictable nature of his behavior.

As he continued walking, the crowd became more spread out, and his earlier restlessness and uncertainty returned. For a while he stayed close behind a group of about ten or twelve rowdy revelers; but one by one they peeled away from this group, until only three remained together, walking down a narrow and dark alley that few people used. The stranger stopped, and for a moment, appeared deep in thought; then, showing clear signs of distress, he quickly took a path that led us to the edge of the city, into neighborhoods completely different from those we had walked through before. This was the most wretched part of London, where everything showed the worst signs of terrible poverty and desperate crime. In the faint light of a random lamp, we could see tall, old, rotting wooden buildings swaying as if about to collapse, leaning in so many random directions that you could barely make out any walkway between them. The cobblestones were scattered everywhere, pushed out of place by thick weeds growing wild. Disgusting filth rotted in the blocked drains. The entire area reeked of decay and abandonment. Still, as we moved forward, the sounds of human activity gradually grew stronger, and eventually we saw large groups of London's most desperate people stumbling back and forth. The old man's energy sparked back to life, like a lamp that flickers just before it dies. Once again he walked forward with a spring in his step. Suddenly we turned a corner, a bright burst of light hit our eyes, and we found ourselves standing in front of one of those massive neighborhood shrines to excess—one of the palaces dedicated to the demon Gin.

It was almost dawn, but a crowd of miserable drunk people still pushed in and out of the gaudy entrance. With a half-scream of joy, the old man forced his way inside, immediately returned to his original behavior, and walked back and forth without any clear purpose among the crowd. He hadn't been doing this for long, however, when a rush toward the doors showed that the establishment was closing for the night. What I saw on the face of this strange person I had been watching so persistently was something even more intense than despair. Yet he didn't hesitate in his course, but with frantic energy, immediately retraced his steps back to the heart of mighty London. He fled for a long time and quickly, while I followed him in complete amazement, determined not to give up an investigation that now completely absorbed my interest. The sun rose as we continued, and when we reached once again that most crowded marketplace of the busy city, the street of the D— — Hotel, it showed a scene of human activity and bustle hardly less than what I had witnessed the evening before. And here, for a long time, amid the constantly growing confusion, I continued my pursuit of the stranger. But as usual, he walked back and forth, and during the day never left the chaos of that street. And as the shadows of the second evening approached, I became exhausted to the point of death, and stopping directly in front of the wanderer, stared at him intently in the face. He didn't notice me, but continued his serious walk, while I, no longer following, remained lost in thought. "This old man," I said finally, "represents the essence and spirit of profound crime. He refuses to be alone. He is the man of the crowd. It would be pointless to follow him further, for I will learn nothing more about him or his actions. The most evil heart in the world is a more disgusting book than the 'Hortulus Animæ,' and perhaps it is one of God's great mercies that 'er lasst sich nicht lesen.'"

THE END

Thank You For Reading

You've Just Read a Piece of the Greatest Library Ever Rebuilt

Thank you for reading.

This book is one of thousands we're restoring, reimagining, and translating as part of the **Modern Library of Alexandria** — a global movement to preserve and share humanity's most important ideas.

What was once lost to fire and time is now rising again — not just as memory, but as living, breathing knowledge, freely accessible to all.

What You Can Do Next:

- **Keep Reading.**

    Discover more legendary works — in beautiful print, audiobook, or digital form — at LibraryofAlexandria.com.

- **Build Your Own Library.**

    Every title is available as a paperback, hardcover, or collectible boxset — at true printing cost. Craft a personal library worthy of display.

- **Spread the Light.**

    Share this book. Tell others about the movement. Help us translate every timeless work into every language, so no reader is ever left behind.

By finishing this book, you've already taken part in something extraordinary.

Join us at LibraryofAlexandria.com

Together, we're rebuilding the greatest library the world has ever known.

With appreciation,

The Modern Library of Alexandria Team

Visit:
www.libraryofalexandria.com
Or scan the code below: